GYMNASTICS

Joe Herran and Ron Thomas

CHELSEA HOUSE
PUBLISHERS
A Haights Cross Communications Company
Philadelphia

This edition first published in 2004 in the United States of America by Chelsea House Publishers, a subsidiary of Haights Cross Communications.

Chelsea House Publishers
1974 Sproul Road, Suite 400
Broomall, PA 19008-0914

The Chelsea House world wide web address is www.chelseahouse.com

Library of Congress Cataloging-in-Publication Data

Herran, Joe.
    Gymnastics / Joe Herran and Ron Thomas.
    p. cm. — (Action sports)

    Includes index.
    Contents: What is gymnastics? — Gymnastics gear — Gymnastics apparatus — Gymnastics safety — Skills and techniques — In competition — Gymnastics champions — Then and now — Related action sports.
    ISBN 0-7910-7534-6
    1. Gymnastics—Juvenile literature. [1. Gymnastics.] I. Thomas, Ron, 1947– II. Title.
    III. Series: Action sports (Chelsea House Publishers).
    GV461.3.H47 2004
    796.44—dc21

                                                            2003001180

First published in 2003 by
MACMILLAN EDUCATION AUSTRALIA PTY LTD
627 Chapel Street, South Yarra, Australia, 3141

Associated companies and representatives throughout the world.

Copyright © Joe Herran and Ron Thomas 2003
Copyright in photographs © individual photographers as credited

Edited by Renée Otmar, Otmar Miller Consultancy Pty Ltd, Melbourne
Text and cover design by Karen Young
Illustration by Nives Porcellato and Andy Craig
Page layout by Raul Diche
Photo research by Legend Images

Printed in China

Acknowledgements

The author and the publisher are grateful to the following for permission to reproduce copyright materials:

Cover photograph: Sabina Cojocar of Romania performing a spectacular backflip, courtesy of Reuters.

AP/Wide World Photos, p. 27 (right); Australian Picture Library/Corbis, pp. 28, 30; Getty Images, pp. 4, 5 (bottom), 13, 25, 29, 30; Manningham DISC center, pp. 6, 7, 9, 11, 12, 14, 15, 16, 18, 19; Reuters, pp. 5 (top), 5 (center), 17, 20, 21 (top), 22, 23, 24, 26, 27 (left); Sporting Images, p. 8.

While every care has been taken to trace and acknowledge copyright, the publisher tenders their apologies for any accidental infringement where copyright has proved untraceable. Where the attempt has been unsuccessful, the publisher welcomes information that would redress the situation.

CONTENTS

INTRODUCTION

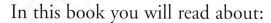

In this book you will read about:

- the different forms of gymnastics
- gymnastics **apparatus** and gear
- safety measures used to keep gymnasts safe
- gymnastics skills and techniques
- gymnastics competitions and how they are judged
- some of the top Olympic gymnasts in competition today
- the history of the sport since ancient times.

In the beginning

In ancient Greece gymnastic activities such as rope climbing, throwing, jumping and wrestling were part of a soldier's training. Later, the Romans added the first apparatus, a wooden horse, called a vault, which was used to teach the soldiers to mount and dismount their horses quickly. In the Middle Ages gymnastics skills were used by troupes of traveling acrobats who included tumbling, juggling and other gymnastics skills in their acts to entertain people in the villages they visited.

During the 18th and 19th centuries gymnastics was a part of training for the German army.

Gymnastics today

Gymnastics was one of the sports included in the first modern Olympic Games, at Athens in 1896. During this Olympic competition just 18 male gymnasts from five countries competed in events that were staged in the center of the athletics field. This established gymnastics as an international sport.

 **Warning** This is not a how-to book for aspiring gymnasts. It is intended as an introduction to the exciting world of gymnastics, and a look at where the sport has come from and where it is heading.

WHAT IS GYMNASTICS?

Gymnastics consists of exercises which develop flexibility, strength and agility. All gymnastic movements are made up of rolls, jumps, springs, balances, turns and landings. There are five main types of gymnastics and the basic movements of gymnastics are common to all.

Artistic gymnastics

Artistic gymnastics is performed on various apparatus. The sport became popular internationally after it was included as an event at the first modern Olympic Games in 1896.

Sports acrobatics and sports aerobics

Sports acrobatics and sports aerobics are performed by male and female gymnasts. These forms are a combination of dance and gymnastic skills, and require pairs or teams of gymnasts to work together to perform **routines**.

Rhythmic gymnastics

Rhythmic gymnastics is a dance-like form of gymnastics for females. The gymnasts perform with hand apparatus such as balls, ropes, hoops, ribbons and clubs.

General gymnastics

General gymnastics is a non-competitive form of gymnastics for people who want to stay fit.

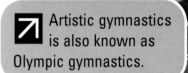

↗ Artistic gymnastics is also known as Olympic gymnastics.

↗ Gymnastics can be enjoyed by pre-school children and adults alike.

↗ Rhythmic gymnastics became an Olympic event in 1984.

5

GYMNASTICS GEAR

Women's clothing

The leotard

Women gymnasts wear a **leotard** that hugs the body. The clothing follows the line of the body so that the body shape and positioning can be seen by coaches during training and by judges during competition. The coaches watch for mistakes so that they can be corrected, while the judges look to award points for good body shape and positioning.

Hair tie

Leotard

Hair ties and clips

Gymnasts must look neat and tidy. Female gymnasts must keep their hair out of their eyes while performing. Gymnasts with long hair wear it pulled back in a pony tail with a hair tie or clip it in place with hair clips.

Men's clothing

Men gymnasts also wear clothing to follow the line of the body so that the body shape can be seen by coaches and judges. A sleeveless leotard is worn during training and competition, with pants or shorts. Shorts are worn for floor and **vaulting** exercises, but men gymnasts are required to wear pants when performing on apparatus such as the rings.

Shoes and socks

Most gymnasts perform in bare feet. However, specially made shoes with non-slip soles may be worn on the floor area, vault or beam. Non-slip socks can be worn instead of shoes.

Handguards

Handguards, also called grips, are worn to help the gymnast get a good grip on the apparatus. They also help to prevent painful blisters. Wrist straps on the handguards give support to the wrist.

Chalk

Gymnasts apply **chalk** to their hands and sometimes to their feet. The chalk prevents the hands from becoming sticky with perspiration and slipping during performance.

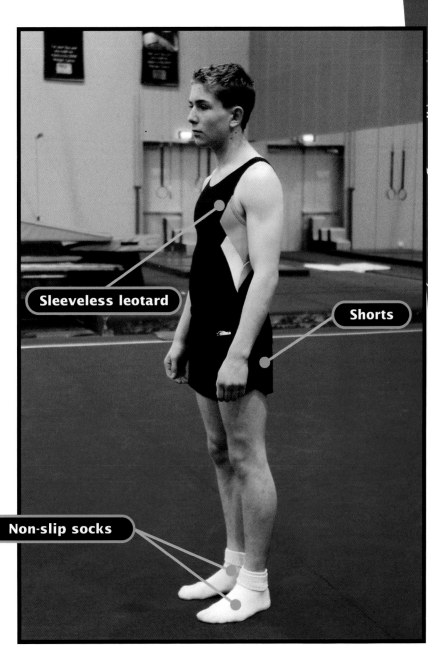

Sleeveless leotard

Shorts

Non-slip socks

GYMNASTICS
APPARATUS

Artistic gymnasts use a variety of equipment on which they jump, hang, somersault and swing. The equipment is known as gymnastics apparatus. The basic equipment required for artistic gymnastics is:

- a 40-foot × 40-foot (12-meter × 12-meter) square mat for floor exercise
- a horizontal (or high) bar that is about 9 feet (2.75 meters) from the top of the mat
- asymmetrical (uneven) bars; the lower bar is about 5 feet (1.5 meters) high while the higher one is just under 8 feet (2.4 meters) high
- two wooden rings suspended on wires about 8.5 feet (2.6 meters) above the floor
- parallel bars set 16.5 to 20.5 inches (42 to 52 centimeters) apart and 6.4 feet (1.95 meters) from the floor

- a **vault horse** set lengthways and 4.4 feet (1.35 meters) high for men, and set sideways at a height of 3.9 feet (1.2 meters) for women
- a **pommel horse**, which is like a vault horse with two handles
- a **springboard** to help the gymnast gain the speed and height needed to perfom a vault
- a balance beam, 16.4 feet (5 meters) long, about 4 inches (10 centimeters) wide and about 3.9 feet (1.2 meters) from the floor
- mats designed to be used with these specialized pieces of equipment.

This arena has been set up with gymnastics apparatus for a competition.

Safety and training equipment

Training mats

Training mats, often called crash pads, are thick pads that absorb the shock of landings. They are especially important when a gymnast is learning a new move or routine, when a poor landing is likely to be made.

Landing pits

Pits are constructed below floor level and are filled with blocks of foam rubber, usually to floor level. They give the gymnast an ideal landing area.

ACTION FACT

The pommel horse was used in the Middle Ages by armored knights who were learning to ride and joust with lances.

LANDING PIT

GYMNASTICS
SAFETY

Gymnasts should follow these basic rules to keep themselves and others safe and injury-free:

- wear proper gymnastics clothing
- remove jewelery
- tie back long hair
- warm up to avoid strains and other injuries
- practice lead-up (simpler) moves when learning newer, more difficult moves
- work within their personal limits and build up their skills over time when learning a new movement
- make sure that mats are set up properly, with no spaces between them
- check apparatus to make sure it is set up properly with plenty of space between pieces
- practice new and risky movements only when a coach or a **spotter** is present.

Spotting

A spotter is a person who helps the gymnast perform movements and balances correctly. The spotter's job is to protect the gymnast from injury by slowing the fall of a performer.

A good spotter:

- gives some assistance to guide the gymnast through the movement
- makes sure the gymnast is in the best position to do the movement
- gives less assistance as the gymnast improves.

Warming up

Before gymnasts compete, they must prepare their bodies for the hard work that is to follow. Warming-up exercises increase the gymnast's heart rate and breathing, and loosen muscles and joints to help prevent injuries. Warming-up activities include jogging, skipping and running, as well as stretching exercises for the arms, shoulders, legs and back. The joints at the wrists, elbows, hips, knees and ankles should also be exercised during the warm-up. Gymnasts usually wear warm clothing such as a track suit while warming up.

CALF STRETCH

The gymnast stands with one foot about 3 feet (a meter) in front of the body, bends the leading leg and leans forward.

STRETCH

The gymnast lies on the back with legs outstretched. The gymnast bends one knee up to the chest and lifts the head and shoulders off the ground.

SKILLS AND TECHNIQUES

The basics

The basic skills that all gymnasts learn before beginning work on any of the apparatus are:

- shapes
- balances
- headstands
- handstands
- jumps and leaps
- **rotations**.

Shapes

The shapes that a gymnast makes with the body are called positions. The beginning gymnast must learn to make a correct shape and then move from one position to another smoothly.

- **Back support position**
  The gymnast lies flat on the floor with hands flat on the ground beside the body. By tensing the body and straightening the arms, the hips are raised and the gymnast forms a straight line from toes to head. The chin is up and the neck is straight.

- **Front support position**
  The gymnast, with arms straight and hips raised, forms a straight line from head to toes facing the floor.

The back and front support positions develop shoulder and arm strength.

BACK SUPPORT POSITION

FRONT SUPPORT POSITION

Balances

A balance is a shape that is made and held for about ten seconds. For good balance work, the gymnast needs good posture, excellent muscle control, flexibility and strength.

- **Shoulder stand balance**

    The gymnast lies flat on the ground with the hands palms-down beside the body. Pushing the arms against the floor, the gymnast bends the knees and lifts the legs to balance the body on the shoulders.

- **V-sit balance**

    The gymnast begins in a sitting position with hands on the floor, behind the body, and the legs bent at the knees, forming a V shape. The legs are raised so that the body forms a V shape. The legs are straight and the toes are pointed. A more difficult V-sit is one where the gymnast lifts the arms off the mat and outwards from the body.

- **Knees and elbows, or squat hand balance**

    Starting in a squat position with legs outside the arms, the gymnast rocks forward into position with both hands on the ground, hips raised and the feet off the ground. The knees rest on the elbows and the toes are pointed.

The V-sit is a move often included in a beam routine.

Headstands and handstands

A gymnast must learn to balance on both the head and the hands, because headstands and handstands are an important part of many gymnastic routines. There are different ways to perform a headstand. These are the tuck headstand and the toe-walk headstand.

- **Tuck headstand**

  The gymnast forms a triangle with the forehead and hands, which are flat on the floor, about shoulder-width apart. The gymnast lifts the hips up above the head and raises the feet into a tuck position. From here the gymnast straightens the legs into an upright headstand.

- **Toe-walk headstand**

  From a crouch position, the gymnast places the hands and forehead on the floor to form a triangle. Slowly, the gymnast walks the toes in closer to the hands to raise the hips above the head. The gymnast then pushes down on the hands and raises the legs into the air.

↗ When performing a headstand correctly, the gymnast always balances on the forehead.

↗ When performing a toe-walk headstand, the gymnast balances on the hands and forehead and walks the toes in toward the hands.

• Handstand

The handstand is an important part of the **sequence** of moves performed in competition floor exercises, bar, beam work, rings and vaults. There are many ways to learn a handstand. With the hands on the ground and arms straight, the gymnast kicks the legs up, one after the other, and holds them together with toes pointed. Another way is to take a long step forward from a standing position with arms stretched overhead, and bending the front leg, to place the hands on the floor. The front leg is straightened as the back leg is kicked up into the handstand position.

↗ A spotter helps the gymnast learning a handstand to find the right position and holds on until the gymnast can balance.

Jumps and leaps

The springboard is used to help a gymnast gain speed or height for a vault or to get onto an apparatus. To get used to the springboard, a beginning gymnast practices the straight jump. Starting with a short run-up to the springboard, the gymnast jumps onto it about 8 inches (20 centimeters) from the end, springs high with arms raised and lands on both feet about 20 to 35 inches (50 to 90 centimeters) in front of the take-off point.

- **Star jump**
  The gymnast takes off from the springboard and stretches arms and legs to form a star shape, before landing with feet together and with the arms at the sides of the body.

STAR JUMP

To get the best spring, the gymnast tries to land on the highest point of the springboard.

- **Squat jump**

  The gymnast takes off from the springboard and brings the knees up to the chest to form a tuck position, before landing with feet together and with the arms at the sides of the body.

- **Straddle pike jump**

  As the gymnast takes off from the springboard, the arms and legs are extended forward to form a pike position, with the body bent forward so the hands touch the toes, before landing with feet together and with the arms at the sides of the body.

- **Split leap**

  The gymnast springs from one foot and lands on the opposite foot without the use of a springboard. The move begins with a run-up to gather speed before the gymnast takes off from one foot and does the splits in the air, landing on the other foot.

↗ This gymnast is performing a split leap during a rhythmic gymnastics routine.

Rotations

Rotations are used in a gymnastics routine to link a variety of shapes and movements. They are used in floor exercises and on the balance beam. Rolls and **cartwheels** are two ways that jumps and flips in a sequence can be linked.

- **Forward roll**

  The gymnast starts in the squat position, balancing on the balls of the feet with hands outstretched. The hands are placed on the floor and the gymnast pushes off with the feet while tucking the head in to the chest. The gymnast pushes with the hands as the hips roll over the shoulders to finish in the squat position.

- **Backward roll**

  The backward roll is a forward roll in reverse. From the squat position, the gymnast rolls backwards and places the hands flat on the ground, close to the ears. Pushing onto the floor, the hips roll over and the gymnast finishes in the squat position.

FORWARD ROLL

• Cartwheel

The gymnast stands and lifts one leg high and straight to the front with toes pointed, then places it forward on the floor. The gymnast bends down, body turned sideways, to place one hand on the floor while at the same time raising the back leg. The gymnast rocks over onto the second hand and the hips pass above the shoulders. The gymnast pushes off the floor with the first hand as the leading foot lands. The cartwheel finishes with both feet apart on the floor and with arms out straight.

A cartwheel looks best when the gymnast's legs are wide apart.

Beyond the basics

The handspring

A gymnast who can hold a handstand is ready for the **handspring**. The handspring is one of the first flying movements a gymnast might learn. Beginning with a short run forward, the gymnast raises the arms then lowers them as they bend to touch the floor. The arms are bent slightly and the legs are kicked rapidly up and over. The gymnast pushes with shoulders and arms to spring and land with feet together, knees slightly bent and arms outstretched.

The handspring vault

The gymnast uses the springboard to gain height over the vault. The hands are placed at the far end of the vault, then the gymnast flips the body over to perform the handspring, before landing with knees slightly bent.

↗ The gymnast hits the springboard at full speed to gain height, in order to reach the end of the vault.

The backflip

From a standing position, the gymnast falls backwards with knees bent and arms overhead. The gymnast then jumps back, straightening the legs and arching the back to bring the hands over and down to the floor.

Forward somersault

The gymnast runs forward and jumps high, with arms stretched upwards. In flight, the gymnast grabs hold of the legs and folds the body into a tuck position and rotates in a somersault. The legs are stretched out for the landing and the arms are forward.

↗ A spectacular backflip by Sabina Cojocar of Romania, at the Brisbane Goodwill Games.

FORWARD SOMERSAULT

IN COMPETITION

International competitive gymnastics is governed by the Fédération Internationale de Gymnastique (FIG) which publishes a "Code of Points" that all coaches and gymnasts must follow. Competing gymnasts perform compulsory routines with a series of set movements on each apparatus, as well as voluntary routines in which each gymnast is free to choose the movements they will perform. Points are awarded by judges for the difficulty of the routine, for how well each movement is performed and for how smoothly the routine flows.

Competitions are held in an arena where all the required apparatus is set up correctly, with plenty of space between them. The gymnasts move around the arena, performing on each apparatus. In international competition there are four events for women and six events for men.

Women's events

Balance beam

A balance beam routine lasts for 70 to 90 seconds. The gymnast performs tumbles, leaps, spins and turns on the narrow beam.

↖ A gymnast performs a graceful **arabesque** on the balance beam.

ACTION FACT

Larisa Latynina (Ukraine, formerly part of the USSR) has won a record number (18) of Olympic gymnastics medals.

Asymmetrical bars

A routine on the asymmetrical or uneven bars includes giant swings, twists, release and catch movements, as well as somersaults and handstands. The gymnast moves from the high bar to the low bar and back again. To finish, the gymnast lands with both feet on the floor, with knees slightly bent.

The vault

The gymnast runs up to the springboard and jumps from it, up and over the vault horse, which is set sideways, to land with both feet on the floor and arms outstretched. The vault event takes just a few seconds.

Floor exercises

A floor-exercise routine includes somersaults, leaps, balances and holds, as well as spinning and turning movements to show off the gymnast's agility, flexibility and strength.

↗ Women gymnasts choose a musical accompaniment for their floor-exercise routines.

Men's events

The pommel horse

The pommel horse is like a vault horse with two curved handles, called pommels. The gymnast jumps onto the pommel horse and moves up and down it using swinging, circling and scissors movements in a routine that lasts about 25 seconds. Points are lost if the gymnast stops or falls off the horse. However, a gymnast who falls can get back on the horse and complete his routine.

The rings

After being lifted onto the rings by his coach or spotter, the gymnast performs swings and handstands. To finish, the gymnast lets go of the rings and lands, feet together and with arms by his sides.

↘ The gymnast must use all parts of the pommel horse in his routine.

Parallel bars

The gymnast moves above, below and across the bars, using just one or both hands. The routine may include hangs, swings and balances to show off the gymnast's strength and balance.

Horizontal bar

During the routine, the gymnast performs giant swings, full circles around the bar and spectacular releases and grabs, using one, both or no hands.

The vault

The gymnast runs up to the springboard and jumps up and over the vault horse, which is set lengthways, to land with both feet on the floor and arms outstretched.

Floor exercises

The gymnast shows off his agility, flexibility and strength in a rhythmic routine which includes tumbles, spinning and turning movements, somersaults, leaps and balances. The routine must last not less than 50 seconds and no more than 70 seconds.

↗ Only the gymnast's hands may touch the apparatus, and the rings should not swing during the performance.

Gymnasts train for many years to reach the top level in world competition. Although there are gymnastics federations and clubs throughout the world, some of the strongest artistic gymnasts come from Russia, Romania and China. Gymnastics competitions are held around the world on the local level as well as in world-class competition. Artistic and rhythmic gymnastics are important events in the summer Olympic Games.

GYMNASTICS CHAMPIONS

↗ Svetlana Khorkina

- Born January 19, 1979, Russia
- One of the most successful Russian gymnasts and a world champion
- Tall and elegant with a unique style

Career highlights

- Won a gold medal on the Uneven bars and a silver medal as a member of the Russian artistic team at the Atlanta Olympics in 1996
- Won the Individual All Around World Championship in 1997
- Won the Individual All Around European Championships in 1998 and 2000
- Won a gold medal on the Uneven bars, a silver medal as a member of the Russian artistic team and a silver medal for her Floor-exercise routine at the Sydney Olympics in 2000
- Won the Individual All Around Title World Championships in 2001

↗ Simona Amanar

- Born October 7, 1979, Romania
- Began training as a gymnast at age 6
- Favorite apparatus is the vault
- First competed internationally at the 1992 Junior European Championships

Career highlights

- Member of Romanian team, winner of the Junior Team Championships in 1992
- Won the Vault event at the World Championships in 1995
- Won the Vault and Uneven-bars events at the European Championships in 1996
- Won a gold medal, a silver medal and two bronze medals at the Atlanta Olympics in 1996
- Won the Vault event at the World Championships in 1997
- Won a gold medal and a bronze medal at the Sydney Olympics in 2000

↗ Aleksei Nemov

- Born May 28, 1976, Russia
- One of the most successful Russian male gymnasts in history

Career highlights

- Won a gold medal as a member of the Russian artistic team, a gold medal in the Vault event, a silver medal in the Individual All Around event and bronze medals in the Floor-exercise, Pommel-horse and High-bar events at the Atlanta Olympics in 1996
- World Champion, Floor exercise and Pommel horse in 1999
- Won a gold medal in the All-Around and Horizontal-bar events, a silver medal in the Floor-exercise event and bronze medals for the Pommel horse, Parallel bars and as a member of the Russian artistic team at the Sydney Olympics in 2000

↗ Shannon Miller

- Born March 10, 1977, Edmond, Oklahoma
- Began gymnastics at age five
- Has won more Olympic and Championship medals than any other male or female American gymnast

Career highlights

- Won two silver medals at the World Championships in 1991
- Won two silver medals and three bronze medals at the Barcelona Olympics in 1992
- World Champion, Uneven bars, Floor exercise, and All-Around in 1993
- World Champion in Beam and All-Around events and silver medalist in Team competition in 1994
- Won gold medals in Beam and as a member of the American Gymnastic Team at the Atlanta Olympics in 1996

THEN AND NOW

1811	1881	1896	1921	1928	1930s
Friedrich Ludwig Jahn established an outdoor gymnastics center in Berlin.	The first gymnastics organization was formed, the Fédération Europeenne de Gymnastique (FEG).	Gymnastics, an event for men only, became part of the first modern Olympic Games; 18 gymnasts from five countries competed.	An international gymnastics organization was formed, the Fédération Internationale de Gymnastique (FIG).	For the first time, women gymnasts competed in Olympic competition at the Amsterdam Games.	George Nissen invented the trampoline.

1928

1936	**1949**	**1964**	**1976**	**1984**	**1992**	**2000**
Rope climbing, Club swinging and Tumbling were discontinued as Olympic gymnastics events at the Berlin Games.	All gymnastics apparatus was standardized so that gymnasts worldwide would be using similar apparatus.	Olympic gymnastics star, Larisa Latynina (Ukraine) competed in her third Olympics. During her career Larisa won 18 Olympic medals: nine gold, five silver and four bronze.	At the Montreal Olympics, Romanian Nadia Comaneci became the first female gymnast in the history of the Games to receive a perfect 10 score.	Rhythmic gymnastics for women became an Olympic sport at the Los Angeles Games.	At the Barcelona Olympics, Vitaly Scherbo of Russia won a record number (six) of gold medals at one Olympic Games.	Trampolining became an Olympic event for men and women at the Sydney Olympics.

1976

1984

RELATED ACTION
SPORTS

Trampolining

Trampolining is a gymnastics sport for both men and women. The trampoline measures 7 feet (2.14 meters) by 14 feet (4.28 meters). Trampolines are made of **nylon** or string about one-quarter inch (6 millimeters) thick. Each competitor performs a routine of jumps, tumbles and somersaults. Judges award points for the height of jumps, the time spent in the air and the difficulty of movements performed while airborne.

Sports aerobics

Sports aerobics is a gymnastics sport which shows off the gymnast's ability to perform combinations of seven basic aerobic dance steps, which are knee lifts, kicks, jacks, lunges, marching, jogging and skipping. The performance, to music, is continuous and the movements are complex. There are events for Individual Women, Individual Men, Mixed Pairs and Trios (groups of three), as well as an event where six gymnasts perform together.

TRAMPOLINING

SPORTS AEROBICS

GLOSSARY

apparatus any piece of equipment used by gymnasts

arabesque a move in which the gymnast leans forward and balances on one leg with the rear leg raised and extended

cartwheels moves in which the hands are placed on the ground sideways, one after the other, with each leg following and the hips passing above the shoulders

chalk a powder made of magnesium carbonate applied by gymnasts to their hands and feet to stop them slipping

handguards leather straps worn on the hands to help the gymnast grip apparatus and prevent blisters

handspring springing off the hands by putting the weight on the arms and using a strong push from the shoulders; can be done either forward or backward, usually a linking movement

leotard a one-piece, body-hugging costume made of two-way stretch material

nylon a synthetic fabric that is very strong and elastic

pommel horse an apparatus that is like a vault horse with handles called pommels

rotations forward or backward movements in a full circle

routines combinations of movements displaying a full range of skills

sequence a number of movements performed one after another

spotter a person who helps a gymnast perform a movement safely while they are learning it

springboard an apparatus on which the gymnast jumps to give them the spring needed to perform vaults and to get onto other apparatus

vault horse a leather-covered block on a stand used for vaulting and other gymnastics exercises

vaulting leaping with the aid of the hands

INDEX